Cros
Alternate Realities

By
Victor Velure

Table of Contents

Introduction

"The energy of mind is the essence of life." -
Aristotle

Thinking is such an everyday occurrence
that we tend to easily forget the amazing
power it really is. To simply be able to form
a thought out of nowhere. By contemplating
on why you have the ability to create any
mental picture, you will begin to see and
feel your own divinity. "Divinity' means
that we are all part of the original source that
makes the Universe possible.

The Hermetic philosophy calls the source
of all energy "The All." Nothing can exist
outside of "The All," and all things are
contained within the mind of "The All." In
The Kybalion, a book on the seven Hermetic
Principles in 1908, goes on to explain that
all things in the Universe are thoughts.

Because "The All" creates mentally, in the mind of "The All." Which is the description of the first Hermetic Principle, called Mentalism.

Vibration is the name of the second Hermetic Principle. It is the link between mind and matter. Since all things in the Universe are thoughts created by "The All," physical matter is just another form of mind. Physical manifestation is really a mental creation with its vibration at a certain frequency to create the illusion of solidity.

Outer manifestations are reflections of the inner mind. Which is the definition of the third Hermetic Principle called Correspondence. And it is Correspondence that explains the Holographic Principle, which means that any portion of any object contains, in a much smaller degree, the entire object. It's like a giant jigsaw puzzle, and any given piece contains the entire puzzle.

This is also where the theory of Infinite Universes comes in. "The All," the source of all existence, also means all of the infinite Universes that already exist. Every human being, you, me, the next-door neighbor and people all over the world are connected to "The All" with our conscious awareness. Going back to the Holographic Universe theory, our conscious awareness contains the entirety of all the infinite Universes.

The whole idea of infinite Universes started to take off back in the 1950s. Researchers were mystified by the characteristics of quantum physics. Quantum physics is a theory to help describe what's going on down to the microscopic level of subatomic particles and atoms. The difference between quantum theory and the older theory of classical mechanics is that quantum theory points to the fact that scientific predictions are subject to the variations of chance. Predicting the odds of reaching a certain outcome, or another, can be achieved, however predicting exactly which outcome will happen could not.

Many outcomes can be predicted but only one result actually happens, and no one could actually explain why. That's when scientists started to second guess the idea that any of the experiments they were conducting has only one single outcome. Scientists started to realize that they were wrong about there being only one possible result of a scientific prediction of odds.

Certain perspectives of the mathematics involving quantum mechanics demonstrate that all the outcomes that are possible are happening simultaneously. And each separate result is within its own Universe apart from the others. If the calculations within quantum physics can predict a particle could be at a certain place or another, then that particular particle exists in one Universe, and the other possible existence of the particle is in a different Universe. What connects each of these Universes is consciousness. There is a version of each person witnessing either one outcome or a different one altogether.

Being conscious, being self-aware, is the key to applying any manifestation method successfully. And according to quantum theory, consciousness is the gateway to infinite realities. By being self-aware, anyone can learn to consciously align their energy to their preferred reality.

The power of manifestation is something that's been taught for thousands of years. Quotes refer to manifesting desires in ancient Biblical scripture such as, "Ask and you shall receive." And as mentioned before, manifestation principles were also taught in Hermetic texts in 2000 BC from ancient Greece and Egypt.

One of these Hermetic writings explains the Principle of Vibration and how the Universe is vibrational and varies in different frequencies. Our Universe around us demonstrates this principle beautifully. At the very start of this Universe, matter was a kind of energy that was only vibrating in the simplest form, which is the element called hydrogen. And for a while, hydrogen was there was. Then, the atoms of this hydrogen started to move closer, becoming denser, and increasing the vibration to the point that it becomes a star.

Now, the next vibrations higher than hydrogen is the element helium. The star eventually gets old enough and eventually explodes. While the star is exploding, it spreads the elements hydrogen and helium out into space. The cycle repeats and the two elements start to gravitate closer and closer together. And when the atoms of the elements hydrogen and helium got dense and hot enough, a new star is created.

Eventually, this vibration reaches the point where lithium is created. This process continued until enough stars have created all the elements necessary to create matter. One of these stars is our Sun and enough bits of matter clumped together and eventually became Earth. Earth now has all the elements that were created, one of which is carbon.

  This process of vibration reaching the next level and making new matter continued until human beings came into existence. What makes humans unique is that each of us has the capability to raise their own vibration, through the power of thought. Another thing that makes us awesome is that we are all made out of stardust. As explained before, it all started with the first star being born.

Chapter One

Conscious Concentration

"Concentration is the secret of strength." -
Ralph Waldo Emerson

With enough frequent repetition of
unconscious thoughts and emotions, an
automatic habit will be formed. It is like a
sort of a software program being formed
inside the brain by doing something over
and over again. And the way to know if you
are running on an old software program is if
the feeling of stressful and fearful emotions
arise. All that's required to stop running on
old programs is to be conscious of it in the
first place.

40% of the human brain consists of the
frontal lobe and it is the symphony leader of
the brain. It is like the CEO, the creative
center of the mind. When someone is
unconscious (meaning not being self-aware)

it is like the boss has left the building and the rest of the brain remains active without any direction. If there is some sort of creative idea, a question or speculating any possibility, that's when the frontal lobe takes charge. Whenever concentration is taking place, the frontal lobe is taking over.

The frontal lobe has access to every area of the brain, so when a question is asked, it activates all the relevant networks of neurons. These neurological networks are formed by experiences and beliefs. Once the frontal lobe accesses these neurons, it creates a new level of mind, and that's when an idea or image pops into mind. And at that moment, the mental image must be embraced emotionally.

This is all relevant to infinite parallel realities in the sense that when the brain is accessing information, it is getting it from its conscious access to the infinite Universes already in existence. The brain actually doesn't come up with ideas. It accesses them like looking for an address to a location that already exists. Once someone emotionally embraces the outcome, that person is essentially living in that parallel reality.

The key is to hold onto the vision without any resistance, any contrary thoughts. Naysayers may try to knock you off course with their cynicism. That's why it is best to keep things as secretive as possible. If the vision is maintained and felt emotionally, that person is living in that preferred specific reality. The changes are just very subtle at first.

If you or anyone else wonder why life hasn't changed for the better, it may be because of certain thinking habits. Most of the time people think in a habitual way. Also, we tend to react and do the same things, allowing ourselves to get overwhelmed by the same emotions. All the while, these people are secretly hoping for things to change in their lives.

The overall thoughts, emotions, and actions of a person are called personality. And it is the personality that creates a certain reality. The chain reaction of thought, action, and manifestation is usually the same. First, the same thought is being entertained, then it leads to the same usual choices, which then leads to the overall behavior as exactly the same. And that is why the experiences are the same as before, it creates the same emotional reactions, which then encourages the same thoughts.

In order to break out of this loop, the first step is to learn how to be aware of the self. Then to learn how to be concentrated on a reality that is preferred. Soon enough, decisions and behaviors will change. Eventually leading to different experiences and emotional reactions.

One hurdle still needs to be addressed to maintain a new chain of cause and effect, and that is the uncomfortable feeling of the unknown and uncertainty. It really takes trust to maintain enthusiasm in the face of existing unwanted current circumstances. This is when it is beneficial to be reminded that thoughts are things (Mentalism) and the feeling the thought evokes is the first physical proof of manifestation (Vibration). The unpredictable, not knowing exactly what's going to happen next, is the moment where the Universe takes over (Correspondence.)

Knowing the minute details of how things will manifest into physical fruition are not necessary. Setting an intention, concentrating, self-awareness of thoughts and emotions, and seizing the intuition, inspired action, and signs given by the Universe is our part in the process. Things just start to work out on their own. With enough awareness, it will be witnessed over and over again. Which then leads to more faith and enthusiasm.

The real crossroad of neuro-science and infinite parallel Universes is the human brain's neurological networks, as briefly discussed earlier. The brain has these little branch-like structures that wire to other branch-like structures with every thought and every experience. It is like a lightning bolt connecting two stems within these neurological networks forming new ones with new thoughts and experiences. So, even if the current physical environment isn't immediately mirroring the new thought-habit, inside the brain the network is changed in the way it would look if the experience already happened.

To be able to tell if the brain has already crossed over to a certain reality, the evidence will be the feelings within the body and upon the skin. That is why it is necessary to embrace the preferred reality emotionally. As if you have fallen in love, and nothing can keep the object of affection out of your mind. So if you are waiting for money to feel wealthy, you are going about things in a backward direction. The same thing goes for needing a person's affection to feel lovable.

Thoughts provide the electrical charge and emotions produce the magnetic charge. Being self-aware of emotions is how to gauge whether or not someone is moving into a preferred reality. It sends a signature electromagnetically, and every atom is influenced by it. Concentration is another word for dedication, dedicating mental focus towards a preferred reality.

This is where meditation comes in, it helps with mental concentration. The word meditation means to familiarize oneself with something. And it is the thoughts unconsciously running in the mind that's necessary to become familiarized with. That is when the automatic habitual responses of thoughts and emotions will be known.

Once this self-awareness becomes more of an automatic habit, there is no returning to the old self again. The brain is now structured with new neurological networks to mirror the preferred reality. The process of reinvention is something that can be done this very instant. Sustaining a thought in awareness creates real physical changes, starting from within the brain.

Nikola Tesla's Concentration

Nikola Tesla had a very intense imagination ever since he was a boy. The intensity of the flashes of images and lights were blinding and came without warning. They would just appear, suddenly before his eyes. If someone uttered a word to him during a conversation that reminded him of something, it could trigger an image so life-like that he found it difficult to distinguish if what he saw was real or not. At first, he felt anxious about this mental ability, but he then learned how to deal with it.

This ability Tesla had actually stimulated his mind and helped him become the genius inventor that he was. He eventually was able to visualize every little single detail of his inventions all within his mind. Before ever needing to write anything down. Tesla would conduct actual test-runs of his inventions within his mind. And he would be able to diagnose any kind of problem the machine might've had.

Nikola Tesla's visualization method is the perfect example of how concentrated you must be to be able to manifest an alternate reality. The mental image has to be more real than the surrounding physical environment. Then the imagination takes on a life of its own. New images emerge that relate to the visualization and gives it more life.

This method that Tesla used led to the entire world changing for the better. He helped make Alternating Current Electricity accessible worldwide. It made so many things possible for humans, things no one could do before. Tesla's patents were allegedly used by Marconi to conduct the first wireless transmission.

Any image consistently sustained within any mind will physically manifest. Concentrating on one thing can be difficult for some. Especially when so many thoughts are coming and going. Before holding a thought in mind, it is best to prepare yourself first. Just like warming up before a game.

Clearing the mind of all thoughts creates the space, some room for the mental image to be placed. It's like when someone is just staring out into nothingness, with a complete blank in their head. It is in those moments when it is best to start focusing on the intention. Because in those moments there are no conflicting thoughts to interrupt the manifestation.

Like listening to the radio with mostly static noise. The static noise represents the multiple conflicting thoughts going on inside the head. When the mind is first clear, then focused on only one thought, it is like the radio dial tuning in exactly on the spot that receives a clear broadcast of sound.

During day to day, moment to moment life, it is inevitable to come across things that may scatter your mental focus. That is when it helps to live everyday life like a passionate inventor like Nikola Tesla. When he was in a focused flow, he may have gotten distracted here or there, but he always went back to the invention and continued to focus. And when he was visualizing his inventions, he was so concentrated that the rest of the world disappeared in those moments.

It becomes so much easier to concentrate on an intention if the focus is on the beautiful qualities of the intention. Like falling in love with someone. It's a magnetic force that attracts the love-struck individual's mind to focus on the beauty. And in those moments it is like time has stood still, and nothing else exists.

A quote from The Bible sums up this concept beautifully in Philippians 4:8, in the New Living Translation. "And now, dear brothers and sisters, one final thing. Fix your thoughts on what is true, and honorable, and right, and pure, and lovely, and admirable. Think about things that are excellent and worthy of praise." The emphasis here is "fix your thoughts."

Viewpoints of Reality

The way anyone looks at the world around them greatly affects what is manifested. Each mental viewpoint has a corresponding reality within the Universe. If the viewpoint is maintained, it creates a path towards a specific reality. Some may think that a mental viewpoint is just an illusion, but the truth is, the viewpoint in mind is the actual view of an already existing reality. If there is a certain thing in life that is unwanted, the power of self-awareness will eventually dissolve it.

Then, a better viewpoint can replace the unwanted viewpoint, until it becomes an automatic habit. Starting out with something small can help build trust in being able to manifest deliberately. Sustaining a thought of something random like a cup of coffee, a piece of gum or a yellow rubber duck will eventually lead to some sort of physical reflection in reality.

Someone may offer a free cup of coffee, for example, or a yellow rubber duck may be seen in an unexpected place. It's in those moments of unexpectedly coming across a sign or physical manifestation that gives rise to trusting yourself and the Universe to be able to manifest mind into matter. When starting out with small random things, there is usually no resistance whatsoever to such objects in the first place.

It's when we try too hard and overwork ourselves that creates resistance. If it matters too much to someone, when it is too serious, then most likely a series of unwanted events may arise. If anyone needs anything to feel validated in any way, then either the desire will not be manifested, or it will be manifested along with extreme unhappiness. It will feel like an empty victory.

The key is to be self-aware enough to notice the conflicting thoughts and feelings. The inner voices of "yeah right," "it's no use," "it's really not happening, nor will it ever!" The light of consciousness shining on the dark spots of doubt will automatically allow intuition and inspiration to take over. The image is an existing reality, so it is best to visualize the actual viewpoint of being completely inside the imagined reality. Instead of seeing the mental image as if a picture on the wall.

The thought process is such a common thing that people tend to forget the amazing power that really is taking place. It is the ability that enables everyone to create a thought picture in the first place that is the starting point power of all that exists. People don't seem to ever question why it is possible at all to form a thought. Feelings of trust and enthusiasm will emerge with the acknowledgment of having the ability to form a thought within the mind.

Sustaining a thought picture will manifest the corresponding reality. Trying too hard to make things happen slows down the momentum of the physical manifestation, however, genuine trust and enthusiasm can help you reach manifested desires. If it is forced or fake trust and enthusiasm it will not work. What naturally builds enthusiasm, (in other words, vibration) is focusing on any beautiful aspects the desire emphasizes.

Enthusiasm tends to be the main accompanying emotion propelling us to keep going. Taking one step at a time becomes an exciting adventure. It becomes easier to find something in the immediate environment relevant to the overall desire that can be utilized and experience. Instead of feeling tension, enjoyment of the action at hand is felt instead.

What creates this tension is when you want to be somewhere else more than being in the present moment. The remedy for this is to be reminded that the end result exists already. And with the mindset and emotional reactions changed, the physical brain is actually changed as well in the present moment. With the vibrational shift felt within the body and upon the skin, it can be viewed as physical proof of living in the preferred reality already here in the present moment.

Chapter Two

Reacting to Realities

"People are not disturbed by things, but by the view they take of them." - Epictetus

The present moment can be compared to many different highways that are beside each other. Each highway stands for a unique experience, different decisions and options you can act upon. A different version-of-yourself is represented on each highway. The now is the grand crossroad to infinite realities.

Every movement you have made or a decision undertaken, you have entered into an alternate reality. It seems like it is the same, but it is not. There are just a lot of similarities that create the illusion that it is the same reality as before.

Continuing to react in the same way to the current surroundings and situations will only perpetuate the same unwanted things to show up. Your reactions reveal exactly what you are in the process of manifesting. So if you are aware enough, you can decide to react differently to a situation that otherwise would have repeated history again.

Portals to Alternate Realities

"It's not what happens to you, but how you react to it that matters." - Epictetus

By reacting differently, you enter an alternate reality. That means that any moment in time and space that provokes a reaction can be considered a portal to a parallel Universe. But you have to be mindful of your reactions in the first place, in order to deliberately enter a preferred reality. Whenever you can't control your concentration, it is the same thing as being hypnotized by an external force. We always have the power to de-hypnotize ourselves at any time, by simply relaxing in our self-awareness.

The simple act of self-awareness will let anyone know what or who is really dominating the mind. If anything unwanted takes over conscious awareness, it can really slow down progress towards the desired reality. In most cases, it is the outer world of unwanted things that dominates the attention of peoples' inner minds. It actually should be in the reverse order. The inner mind determines what is seen in the outer world.

It is very comparable to the process of developing a roll of film. If someone is taking something undesirable too seriously, it is the same thing as having the developing film inside the mind, created from the external image. To reverse this process, the developing film must be placed out into the external world, which is created from the inner image held in mind. The light of consciousness within lights up what is seen without.

Another analogy that describes the process of the mind-manifesting matter is the Earth's north and south poles. Whenever anyone is sustaining any thought in mind, they are entering into an alternate reality. Which is equivalent to following a compass with the needle pointing north. Once an external event is allowed to dominate your mind, it is like a major planetary pole shift. Now things are heading south, really fast, and it is up to the conscious mind to become self-aware again.

Once any worry is dropped and comfort has restored itself within the mind and body, the surrounding environment will eventually mirror that feeling of relief. The screenplay of reality will be better and the necessary things will make themselves known on their own. This is the meaning of going with the flow. Self-awareness will automatically reveal if there is a misalignment of energy, and it will make the culprit known. Which is usually either a past thought or a current event that is given extra unneeded importance.

Then the next step is to see the past thought or current unwanted event impersonally, as if not important at all. The first sign of physical manifestation is the vibrational shift within. Certain feelings such as relief, trust, and enthusiasm. And while sustaining those thoughts, other physical external manifestations will appear.

This is just like being the main star of a movie. Sustaining a thought and absorbing it as reality, is the spotlight on the life-movie of a certain reality. Acting and reacting to the surrounding environment in trust enthusiasm is playing the part of the starring role as the life movie unfolds. Part of playing the part within the holographic screen of reality is being aware of the outer events acquiring personal meaning, and are relevant to the thought held in mind.

It is not the actor's job to come up with every prop, exact detail and timing of the storyline. That is the job for those who work behind the scenes in charge of the exact details of settings, props, characters and surprising plot twists. If the actor insisted on now things should happen in the movie it would bring a lot of disruption on the set. So by dropping the need to take control of everything, the movie can be made well

Bad Angels

Every good movie has a bad villain to overcome. And there are villains walking on Earth today conducting actual forms of vampirism. In the form of taking energy, instead of actual blood as told in books and seen in movies. And the reason why energy is being robbed in the first place is that these energy vampires rely on it to survive.

Plenty of fictitious novels, cartoons, movies and t.v. shows have shown a scene or image of a good angel on one shoulder and a bad angel on the other. That is a perfect representation of what goes on in the mind when it comes to destructive thinking. There is always the option to start thinking in a healthier way, but the bad angel always comes up with some compelling arguments. When it comes down to it, the bad angel is really telling all lies.

Just like an external energy vampire, there exists an invisible energy vampire sitting on one side of every person's shoulder. The good news is that the light of consciousness also exists on the other side, waiting lovingly and patiently. It is conscious awareness that dissolves the energy vampire, both visible and invisible. It is unconsciousness, not being self-aware, that allows the energy vampire to do what it does to feed off the energy.

The reason why the invisible energy vampire sitting on one shoulder has so much to whisper in your ear is that it knows all of your deepest darkest secrets. By accessing the "shame file" within your brain.

Whatever mistake you've made, rejection suffered, memories of abuse or any fears about the future will be known to this invisible vampire. When someone starts to hear those dark voices of negativity, it is the energy vampire trying to sink its fangs.

The whispers from the invisible bad angel/vampire trigger memories that were actually experienced. So it becomes very easy to get convinced into a destructive way of thinking. Another strategy for you to slay the vampire is by looking upon the negative thoughts in an impersonal way. As if recalling a dream, but feeling relieved that it was "just a dream."

Energy flows through the energy channels within the human body. If you are feeling stressed or depressed, it is because of how closed up the energy channels are. The kind of reality experience is determined by the quality of energy flowing through the body, just like a stained glass window. The colors of light shining through are determined by the colors of the stain glass window.

All it takes to open up the energy channels is to relax in the present moment and to appreciate the beautiful things that are already present in life. The problem is, there are some toxic people out there who don't know how, or don't want to, appreciate anything to increase life energy. It's much easier for them to get energy from other people.

The main goal of an energy vampire is to make you react negatively, to throw you off course. To keep you in an undesirable reality instead of moving toward one that is desired. At least three main types of energy vampires exist, the first kind is called "The Imposing Vampire." This kind of energy vampire uses flattery to dig deeper into your mind and heart, for their own benefit. Just so he or she can figure out how to get energy out of their unsuspecting victim.

Not that it is always a bad thing to be flattered by someone. It is just best to be aware of people's motives as they do so (and you should already know how awesome you are anyway.) For the most part, the flattery is very subtle because it starts out with just giving some attention to the intended victim. A little eye contact, a touch on the shoulder and consistent small talk.

All the while this energy vampire is basically conducting an interview. Just like the book and film, *Interview With the Vampire*, there is a real-life version of that. Except, this time the vampire is conducting the interview to see how he or she can rob vital energy from the victim. The main sign to look out for is the way a person influences your emotions.

The second kind of energy vampire can be called "The Guilt Trip." This kind of person will try to make others feel sorry for them. Just to get whatever it is that they want. And the more the vampire knows about the prey. The more ways they will know how to make them feel guilty.

The Instigator is the name of the third energy vampire. And the strategy of this type of monster is to throw you off balance. They will purposefully say or do something knowing it will hurt or anger you. For anyone to become an energy vampire slayer all it takes is to relax in the light of conscious awareness to shine through the eclipse of an energy vampire. By being relaxed instead of reactive, the vampire can't tap into any energy with its metaphoric fangs.

Sometimes it is a close relative, a work colleague or even a friend that's an energy vampire. It can take some time for someone to see the other's true colors. Instead of a rainbow, darker colors of grey are seen instead. Another adequate visualization for these people is to see them as actual vampires with fangs, making hissing noises like a cat.

What is happening during an energy vampire attack is that the victim is getting its energy sucked out telepathically. Another term for energy vampire is a psychic vampire, or psy-vamp because they do their dirty work psychically. It is like seeing light energy seeping out of a person into the fangs of the vampire, receiving that energy. The truth will set you free once you see the vampire for what is.

If the aura (the surrounding human energy field) were to be visible, two puncture holes can be seen, made by the psy-vamp to suck out the energy. Actual scientific studies have been conducted on this phenomenon. The research was confirmed by the Parapsychology Foundation of New York. The auras of romantic couples were visually observed and photographed.

What the research showed is that when a couple was being harmonious with each other, the aura's strength intensified. But if a couple was being unkind to one another in some way, their auras would constrict and weaken. Certain studies showed that some people know how to tap into the other person's energy on purpose. And by doing so, the victim's aura was documented as getting weaker and smaller as the energy vampire's aura is gaining in strength.

The puncture wounds from the fangs of the vampire can last for a long time as well. It usually happens in the form of rumination in the mind. Recalling thoughts about what the vampire said, did or didn't do. Without enough self-awareness, those puncture wounds will continue to seep away vital energy.

Money in the Moment

It is difficult to want money without getting too possessive over it. When it weighs in the mind more than all the other aspects of life. The key is to learn to be not so dependent upon money as a source of feeling worthy as a person or validated in any way. It is alright to be happy if there is money in the bank. What is not alright is to react with despair and self-hatred if there currently is not enough money.

That is the funny thing about money.
When someone feels wealthy, more wealth
comes pouring in. But if that person were to
allow money worries to taint their mind, all
the wealth starts to slip away. Radiating
thought energy of money worries shifts you
into an unwanted reality of more financial
difficulties.

Fear is such a powerful vibrational
frequency of energy. That's why being
aware of fear arising, in the beginning, is so
beneficial. It will nip the fear in the bud.
Trust is the best ally to have in times like
these. To relax in the present moment,
knowing that it is the gateway and crossroad
to any parallel reality.

Acceptance and trust go hand in hand. To
accept means to allow yourself to be calm
and relaxed in the face of unwanted events
or uncertainty. Relaxing the body, inside
and out, opens up the inner energy channels.
That's when a vibrational shift within the
body will be felt.

The common worldwide belief is that in order to get anything, you need the money first. And because of this erroneous way of thinking, people tend to switch their main goals in life to that of acquiring money only. Money, as an aim in and of itself, causes people to switch into a reality that is far from the one that would bring ultimate happiness and fulfillment.

A deeper look into most wildly successful and rich people will show that they pursued their own goal, not the goal of money. It would have hampered creativity if money was the main goal. And that would make it hard to be able to come up with anything worth making money with in the first place. The money is just an attribute accompanying the journey towards the main goal, which is something other than money itself.

Whenever anyone can continue going after their dreams despite financial conditions, money finds a way towards the person. Money has a funny way of getting into your hand and pocket. Strenuously pursuing money makes money run away and hide. Yet, letting go of money worries while focusing on other things attracts money like a magnet.

It all comes down to what thoughts are being sustained about money, and what reactions are taking place as well. Whenever a certain negative reaction to money happens, there's an opportunity to enter a reality of financial success. By reacting in a positive manner, you enter into a more desirable reality. With enough self-awareness, the habitual reactions will be noticed in the usual places.

One place that may cause an emotional reaction towards money is the ATM. Seeing the money popping out of the machine while the bank balance number goes down. It is like feeling guilty and disappointment in using the machine at all. Instead of that kind of reaction, you can feel excited, and trusting that things are working out in unknown ways at that moment.

Other portals to wealth may be when receiving your paycheck. A lot of times it can seem less than the desired amount (especially after taxes, insurance, FICA and so on.) Instead of reacting as disappointed, be grateful that there's a paycheck at all in the first place. The same process can be applied when receiving bills in the mail.

The Hermetic Pendulum

Money comes and goes, just like ocean tides. When the tide is low it may feel like you're a fish out of water. Bouncing and struggling to reach the water. The tide always comes back again. There is evidence of this in nature.

It is also part of the Hermetic principles of Rhythm and Polarity. *The Kybalion* describes the Principle of Rhythm as," Everything flows, out and in; everything has its tides; all things rise and fall; the pendulum swing manifests in everything;

the measure of the swing to the right is the measure of the swing to the left; Rhythm compensates." This is nothing but good news, especially when it comes to money.

The low tide of not having money is the Pendulum swinging on the opposite side. And in time, it will swing in full force in your direction. And then it will be a high tide of money in the bank. This is also called the Law of Compensation. And if you look closely in your own life, you can see the pattern of how things eventually work themselves out somehow.

The key is to remember this when the Pendulum of Rhythm and Polarity is swinging in the opposite desired direction. Polarity is the Hermetic Principle explains why "the opposite side" exists in the first place. "Everything is dual; Everything has poles; everything has its pair of opposites; like and unlike are the same; opposites are identical in nature, but different in degree; extremes meet; all truths are but half-truths;

all paradoxes may be reconciled." - *The Kybalion*.

This is the second set of good news the Hermetic Pendulum delivers. If a lack of something exists, the abundance of that thing must also exist simultaneously. For example, cold and hot are just different degrees of temperature. Lack of money and abundance of money are both different degrees of prosperity.

If the sun sets, it will rise again. If the tide is low, it will rise again. If your mood is low, it will rise again. If your heart is broken, it will mend again. If you lose your job, another opportunity will open up for you.

It is when people don't hang on long enough who believe that there is no hope whatsoever. It's been said that the people who have decided to end their lives were actually very very close to achieving something great in their lives. Everything in your life is fixable, except if you were to do the irreversible.

Life is an adventure, and it should be lived in that way. It can get very scary sometimes, but it usually is only scary because it is preparing you for something bigger and better. And when that Pendulum of abundance swings your way, it's going to be clear why you had to go through what you went through. The dots will be able to be connected, after the fact. But before that, you need to rely on that gut feeling and follow the inspired action.

Focusing on the solution instead of on the problem is the basis of the Hermetic process called the Law of Polarization. If you are experiencing something unwanted, the opposite must also exist, it is a universal principle. Otherwise, the unwanted experience wouldn't exist in the first place. This is not a matter of trying to force yourself to feel better. It is just a simple reminder of your divine abilities, by just being a conscious entity in the Universe.

If you don't feel better, however, just
remember the Law of Compensation.
Inevitably you will feel better. Sometimes
you just have to let the accumulated
momentum of bad vibrations die down on
their own. It is that momentum that can
easily suck you back into the bad vibrations.
Just remember that it is only dissipating
momentum of unwanted energy.

For example, someone said something rude
to you and now you feel a negative reaction
within you. The Pendulum of your mood is
now in a back-swing, or in terms of tides, a
low tide. If you stay unaware of what is
happening, you will get overly attached to
the situation and the bad feelings
accompanying it. Now you are like a fish
out of water struggling for survival. Saying
things back to the rude person, and
subsequently, wasting more of your time
and energy.

Being caught up in negative reactions to an
external event is the same as being under

hypnosis. It is like the pendulum is dangling in front of your eyes, and it is keeping you in a trance. Sustained self-awareness will protect you from a destructive pendulum's attempt to hypnotize you.

By allowing yourself to relax at the moment, despite what is going on, you will emotionally detach yourself from the unwanted situation. There still will be a momentum of bad vibes, but with self-awareness, you'll notice it dissipate by the moment. Now the pendulum is swinging to the desired direction.

The best part of all this is that each time the Hermetic Pendulum swings back to the desired position, it raises to a higher vibrational level than the one it began with. That means that out of all the ups and downs of life, you'll always end up better off than before. You become wiser, stronger and better equipped to receive your wildest dreams.

Chapter Three

The STREAM

Many times people fall short of manifesting desires because they think that it all stays in their head as just a thought. Or in other words, "only in my dreams". And it can get really frustrating when you are attempting to change the way you feel. The reason is that if you try too hard, it will defeat the purpose. Trying too hard only creates more resistance.

Without bringing all this into the present moment, into the current reality being experienced, it can get really difficult to keep the faith alive. As mentioned many times in this book, our consistent thoughts and reactions in the present moment determine the reality we will eventually experience. And if we keep thinking and reacting the same way to the same things, we will continue living the same undesirable situations.

Any physical movement is a shift in parallel realities. If you move to the left you are now in a different reality than the reality where you turned right. Even down to the molecular level, the reality is shifting as well. No matter how insignificant the movement is. As long as the bodily movement evokes a certain reaction, it is effectively shifting you into a preferred reality.

Words in Action

The words we say have a very powerful force to them. They help us shift into an alternate reality. As long as the words have a positive influence on our vibrational frequency. Trying too hard to believe an affirmation can actually perpetuate the same unwanted reality. So then the question is, "how do I get myself to believe in an affirmation without trying too hard?"

This is where bodily movements come in, to bring life into the affirmations. Merging a physical gesture, or activity to the affirmation in a relevant way will magnetize the words within the affirmation. You do this by finding a metaphorical correlation between physical activity and self-suggestion.

Self-suggestion is what helps elicit a response within you. With self-awareness, you will know whether or not the response is positive or negative. Combining an affirmation with a certain activity will help you be consistent with your thought patterns and reactions to the immediate surrounding environment.

Thoughts in your mind may seem like "just" thoughts. Words spoken out loud or silently in the mind may seem like "just" words. But when you add the element of physical activity within the moment, the energy of the thoughts and words become actual portals to alternate realities. And by adding the element of consistency, the new mindset and daily habits are set in place.

There is real-life symbolism in physical reality and in almost every activity there is in life. The examples are almost endless. Think of how many times you have heard metaphorical statements throughout life. "The world is your oyster," "step up to the plate," "a diamond in the rough," "opportunity knocking," "as easy as pie," "as good as gold," "hit the nail on the head," and so on.

All you have to do is to decide on an everyday activity that contains a symbolic meaning that is relevant to your intention. Then recite the self-suggestion as you carry out the physical activity. This has a way of dehypnotizing yourself of unwanted beliefs and reprogramming your mindset towards a better reality. This method communicates directly to the mind, heart, and soul. Bypassing the bad angel's mal intentions.

For example, while driving in your car, you can simply say, " I drive myself to meet success confidently." Whenever you are flossing your teeth say, " I floss out all bad eating habits from my life." These are just some examples, the key is to customize this in your own way. Be as creative as you can. It all depends on the intention and the physical activity taking place.

To be successful with this manifestation process of combining words and actions, it needs to be consistent. And there are plenty of daily activities that contain a metaphoric and relevant meaning to them. Some of the main activities are hygienic practices, sleeping, walking, arising, eating, driving and so on. Depending on your intention, the actual self-suggestion combined with the daily activity varies.

Finding the main association behind the daily activity to the affirmation is all that is necessary to find the metaphorical meaning to the action. Waking up is associated with realizing or identifying something. So the self-suggestion can be about being "awakened" to money-making opportunities. Hygienic practices relate to purifying and cleansing yourself. The affirmation during these activities can be about "cleansing" yourself from self-limiting beliefs that hold you back from success.

Subconscious Cruise Control

Ever wonder what's the power behind the beating of your heart, what keeps you breathing while asleep at night, and what gives you that inner gut feeling that speaks to you? One name for it is the Subconscious Mind. It's like a bio-computer than can be programmed. Our bodies already come pre-programed to breathe, digest food, sleep and so on. But it's up to us to program the subconscious to help us manifest the life we want to live.

So far in this book, the theory of infinite realities, the Holographic Principle,

Neurology and the Hermetic Principles have been fused together by describing their relevance to manifesting desires. "Now I got to know about this so-called Subconscious Mind?" you may be thinking. The subconscious mind is part of our overall consciousness, and it is the bridge to any reality you desire. Like an iceberg in the ocean, the tip is our conscious awareness, the much larger underwater part of the iceberg is our subconscious.

The subconscious mind is a microcosm of the Universe, due to the Holographic Principle which means that the subconscious contains all there is anywhere and everywhere. And the subconscious gut feeling that the Universe is offering is the Hermetic Principle of Correspondence. By following that gut feeling we enter into a more desirable reality. By repeatedly thinking, speaking and acting in a certain way, your subconscious mind takes you to manifested desires. Like setting your cruise control function in your car while on a long road trip.

Evidence of this has most likely already happened to you. Have you ever missed an exit on a highway, and you didn't realize it until a mile or two later? It's called highway hypnosis, and It is our subconscious mind on cruise control. It takes self-awareness to wake up and realize that you're going the wrong way. Then, it takes a shift in your mindset to eventually witness the shift in reality.

It's what we think, say, feel and do on a consistent basis that programs us to be at the right place, at the right time to meet the things we what to have. Fusing together thoughts, words, feelings, and taking action is the best way to get into the right alignment. And we do that by saying a self-suggestion while performing a certain activity relevant to the self-suggestion.

This method is so effective because it bypasses our internal filter. The space between our conscious and subconscious minds. That's why saying an affirmation alone is not enough. You may reach vibrational alignment for a second, but the internal filter will then say "yeah right!" However, when you physically move and do something about the intention and affirmation, it has a way of releasing the excess resistance built up within the body.

The STREAM of Realities

It might seem like there's a lot to remember when it comes to shifting into a preferred reality. Manifesting a thought into a physical experience becomes easier with the STREAM. It is an acronym that stands for, Sustain a Thought Repeatedly and Exemplify it in the Activities of the Moment. This is a personal reminder to be consistent with the reality shifting process in four ways.

First, to be consistent with your thought process, and second, to make consistent movement characteristic of the intention in mind. Thirdly, It's also a reminder to stay within the present moment awareness to be ready to meet the opportunities already waiting for you. And lastly, it helps you remember to be aware of your reaction because a different reaction means is entering a different reality.

Decide on the biggest intention you have for your life. That mental picture is considered the tip of the manifestation pyramid. It affects the rest of the intentions you have for yourself. Just think of how different your life would be anyway if your wildest dreams come true. Think of all the other aspects and areas of life that would be influenced.

When you Sustain a Thought Repeatedly and Exemplify it in the Activities of the Moment you are "STREAM-ing" along into an alternate reality. At first, it may seem like nothing has changed other than your mindset and how you feel. Which is really the first "physical evidence." But with enough consistency, the evidence will be more physically emphasized. You will begin to see the outer signs from the Universe.

Contemplating on what space is has a way of quieting and stilling the mind. Both outer space, the space around us and within us. Space can be compared to a structure, a field, infinite in size, containing infinite intelligence. It is The holographic screen of reality containing the information for the variation of every possible event that can ever happen. Everything that will be, has been, and what is happening now is all within the holographic screen of reality.

Just like a high definition t.v. screen. Instead of pixels, this screen moves actual physical matter. Everything from the past and future is contained in the screen of reality, and it is held there in place, just like a film reel. Time is really the illusion made when one of these frames is moving in the present moment.

The non-physical part of human existence is equivalent to a remote control that is wirelessly connected to the t.v. screen. If one thing exists in the Universe the polar opposite also exists. So if there is physical existence, there also must be a non-physical existence. And is the non-physical that determines what ends up being physically manifested.

The conscious mind is connected to the holographic screen of reality. Although it may seem like the mind is coming up with ideas, images, and intuitive guidance out of thin air, it really is accessing information from all the infinite realities in existence. Whenever any kind of image comes to mind it is an already existing reality. This also includes dreams and daydreams. They are not illusions, they're a real journey through the infinite realities of the holographic screen of reality.

A reality already exists that contains the outcome of any so-called "missed chances," or "what if's." If anything in this universe moves in any particular direction, a different Universe exists where that one thing moved in a different direction. And a whole different chain of cause and effect will occur.

Cause and Effect (the sixth Hermetic Principle) is not subject to physical movement, the energy of thoughts is what precedes action. A specific thought contains the possibility to materialize a specific reality. Every individual on Earth is manifesting a specific reality at this very moment. And each of these sections of realities contributes to the overall existence of the entire world.

The only way for anyone to truly know what thought energy is being emitted is to pay attention to the inner feelings within the body. The attitude you feel towards things, the world or even yourself. It is like setting specific weather patterns by simply adjusting an attitude. If you wake up in the morning and maintain uplifting thoughts about the day, the rest of the day will be like sunshine and blue skies. If you happen to wake up grumpy and didn't change that thought energy, the day will be wet, cold and stormy.

To recap, the STREAM stands for, Sustain a Thought Repeatedly and Exemplify it in Activities of the Moment. Each thought and each action aligned to that thought is a shift into an alternate reality. The STREAM of realities is like a roll of film. At first, it stays static. Any kind of movement, even down to the molecular level, is the process of each frame moving one by one. Each frame represents an alternate universe, and each frame is linked together as cause and effect.

The screen of reality (what we see and experience) is a structure of infinite intelligence linked together. This means that any problem has a link to the solution anywhere and anytime. The chain of cause and effect moving towards a solution is always in the path of least resistance. With enough patience, the solutions to problems work themselves out.

Present moment awareness also means going with the STREAM of realities. More problems arise when someone resists going with the flow. Therefore, stressing out makes things so much worse. Relaxing and the feeling of trust is the best thing that can be done to make most situations better. Unless the situation requires a fight or flight response to any real physical danger.

The solution already exists, it's just a matter of allowing it to arrive. What that implies is to do whatever the next obvious step is to use what is already available and doing things with ease and no discomfort. And every little decision made, every moment made, is selecting the next link within the chain of cause and effect.

What if the next obvious step isn't so obvious? As explained in the previous chapter, you can use everyday activities with hidden metaphoric meanings, and say a self-suggestion implying that you are manifesting your desire. For example, when washing your hands you can say, "I wash my hands from all things holding me back from manifesting my desires." Making moves, moving your body has a way of releasing endorphins into your body. That's why simple yet consistent exercise is so powerful in influencing a positive change in many areas of life, not just weight-loss.

By reacting to the immediate surrounding as someone who already is living the desired reality is also a manifestation action plan. Learn to be relaxed when dealing with money. Take things impersonally, no matter what. Don't give any power to the things and people who don't deserve it.

Screenplays and Props

Every variation of realities within the screen of reality has specific outer manifestations of the world, and portals for physical matter to move through. The outer manifestations can be called the props of reality and the portals, the screenplay of reality. The farther away one reality seems to another reality, the more differences there will be in the outer manifestations and portals of physical matter. Different screenplays of reality with different props.

The variations of specific realities represent a person's destiny. In the screen of reality, cause and effect are closely linked. The shift to each section of realities is usually very seamless as each reality is being experienced, one after another. The screenplays and props are generally the same within one reality until something happens that changes them. That is when destiny turns towards a different reality.

It's very similar to streaming movies online that you have already seen, and then decide to watch an alternate version that is very similar to the original, but with a different result. Each version of the movie is an alternate reality, and each of the realities is in very close proximity to each other on the screen of reality. It's similar to two trails seemingly parallel to each other in the beginning, but down the road, the two trails are going in different directions entirely.

Just like a couple in love. At first, the small differences may not be a big deal because the passion is still so strong. But if two people share different values, somewhere down the road they will realize they have grown apart. Then they will be wondering "what happened to the passion."

Going back to the movie streaming analogy, if you were to watch a remake of the original movie 20 years later, it may come across as an entirely different interpretation of the original. With new actors, screenplay, and props. A strong sense of things not being the same will be felt and noticed.

The beauty of all this infinite abundance of possible variations of reality is that anyone can begin anywhere, anyplace, no matter what. A chain reaction of cause and effect can start anywhere. A proper mindset and actions can get anyone to start to see their reality correspond to the new energy of thoughts and actions. And in doing so, that person is moving through a reality portal, to that preferred specific reality.

One moment is one Universe, the next moment is another. Just very similar, yet still, it's a different Universe. Every new experience is an alternate reality. Every new haircut, new day, new job and every movement made, is an alternate Universe.

The erroneous assumption is that the changes that are seen are consistent within the same reality. No matter how seemingly irrelevant the movement of physical matter may be, it is really alternate Universes being shifted. A hand moving from one side to the other is moving through multiple Universes that already exist between each side of the hand movement. The conscious mind can view each of the realities so that it makes the transition smooth and seamless. It creates the illusion of only one continuous reality, but it really is not.

The Chain of Cause and Effect

As mentioned earlier in this chapter, this process of getting into the STREAM of realities is the sixth Hermetic Principle. *The Kybalion* refers to it as, "Every Cause has its Effect; every Effect has its Cause; everything happens according to law; chance is but a name for a law not recognized; there are many planes of causations but nothing escapes the law." Thoughts are the Cause, the corresponding physical manifestation is the Effect. Reacting differently to some sort of external provocation changes the vicious cycle of a chain Cause and Effect that is unwanted.

It's a matter of not allowing external forces to be the Cause. The thought energy influences the Hermetic Pendulum to swing in a favorable direction. All of space, in between objects and in between planets. It is

like a system of energy pendulums. Each
pendulum influencing the other, vibrating
and attracting similar frequencies.

To reiterate an example given earlier in this
book, it all starts when you wake up in the
morning. What side of the bed, good or
bad? Are you going to let that inconsiderate
driver in the other car trigger you into road
rage mode? That's not a way to begin your
workday. What happens if a coworker, or
even worse, your boss is rude to you?

Self-awareness will allow you to see what
life path you are on. Decide to relax instead
of reacting, which basically means to accept
the thing first, not fighting against it. The
Universe starts to work in your favor in
those moments of relaxing in your
self-awareness and well-being.

Chapter Four

Synchronicity IS the Secret

"Accept whatever comes to you woven in the pattern of your destiny, for what could more aptly fit your needs?" - Marcus Aurelius

The outer reflection of inner states of mind is a phenomenon that most scientists have completely ignored. A Swiss psychiatrist named Carl Jung started to research this connection between non-physical thoughts and physical reality Jung noticed hundreds of coincidence that occurred, but with no cause that can be seen. Jung used the word "synchronicity" to explain these meaningful coincidences. He gave examples of synchronicity in a lecture he provided called "On Synchronicity."

In one example, Jung saw an inscription of a man that was half fish. Then he had fish for lunch. During a conversation, he heard someone use the phrase "April Fish.' During that afternoon he ran into a former patient he hadn't seen for months and showed him some interesting pictures of fish. After that, in the evening, he saw more fish and sea creatures in embroidery that someone showed him.

The synchronicity wasn't over for Carl Jung just yet. The next morning he had a visit from an old patient of his that he hasn't seen for ten years. And this woman told him of a dream she had the night before of a large fish.

He decided to document the series of meaningful coincidences a few months later. And after he wrote everything down, he decided to go for a walk by the lake which was in front of his home. He ended up seeing a footlong fish laying on the sea wall, and he had no clue how that fish ended up there.

Meaningful coincidences are very hard to ignore and equally hard to explain. It can only be meaningful to the person experiencing the coincidence. The simplest way to define synchronicity is to experience an external event that is relevant to an inner mental state. The relevance within the event usually stands out and is emphasized in awareness.

With enough awareness, anyone can experience similar synchronistic events like the ones Carl Jung experiences. Sometimes the link of smaller, seemingly irrelevant things goes unnoticed. With an alert mind, meaningful synchronistic events become easier to spot. The dots will be easier to connect, after the fact.

Meaningful Messages

"It's just a coincidence, don't look into it so much," and others sayings that are skeptical in nature all are hiding the real truth. And the truth is, every event, every moment and personal encounters with others have meaning. It's just up to each individual to discover the message.

No matter how wonderful or awful a friendship or relationship used to be, or still is, that person is there for a reason. Of course, any awful person must be left alone eventually, especially if physical safety is concerned. That is what the fight or flight response is for. To be clear, violence is not something anyone deserves. The meaningful message is loud and clear in those cases, and that is "run away from this monster!"

Overcoming a toxic relationship can bring so much wisdom and a new outlook on love and life. It can be like a giant mirror exposing any inner weakness that needs to be addressed. Or, it can show the inner strength that has been there all along.

Sometimes the meaningful messages throughout life may not be so apparent at first. A synchronistic event took place but the meaning might not be known until later. Patience is very beneficial to be able to see the meaning behind things. Usually, if not always, the meaning behind events is to evolve in conscious awareness. Also, the meaning behind the synchronistic event is to show you the outer reflection of what is being thought of the majority of the time.

Every thought matters, so it is an accumulation of thought energy that inevitably manifests into something. Whenever someone has the intention to be observant of meaningful messages in the surrounding environment, the environment tends to jumps out towards awareness of any relevant information. Whether it is something a co-worker said that sparked an idea in mind or the news on t.v. relaying some information that can be used in some beneficial way. If something were to stand out in the environment, there is a reason, and it's up to the observer to notice it.

Many times it is the unwanted events that stand out more than anything else. And since it is already in awareness, it perpetuates more unwanted events. The outer environment is reflecting negative things and it seems like there is a momentum that can't be stopped. This is called Murphy's Law, which means, what is feared will happen, does happen.

Other words for fear are importance, seriousness, and excessiveness. Reality conforms to thought energy, so the energy of fear will attract a reality that is unwanted. This doesn't imply that there is no use to care about anything or anyone. It means that when a goal is taken excessively seriously, the universe will bring up the opposite of what is really wanted to balance out that energy.

It is possible to reach a goal, and not entertain thoughts of fear and doubt along the way. It is a sort of balancing act of manifestation. Similar to an inexperienced trapeze performer walking on an elevated rope, without a safety net below. If the rope were to be closer to the ground with a safety net underneath, it's easier to practice walking on the rope without any fear. But the higher the rope, and without the comfort of a safety net below, suddenly, excessive importance and fear take over.

The "safety net," in this case of reaching a goal is the light of conscious awareness. It will light up the dark spots in the mind that are filled with fear. It can be like a fun game. All that has to be done to win over obstacles and fear is to remember to turn on the light of consciousness and let go of taking things way too seriously. The perfect balance is to leave out worry, but still care at the same time.

Vibes Between People

When you think of someone else in a negative way it will emit that thought energy towards that specific person. That person receiving the toxic thought vibrations will perceive them in some way. Like getting a bad vibe while being around each other. And so the reality screenplay becomes one of the tensions or possibly an argument.

Thinking of the beautiful aspects of a person has a way of creating a harmonious balance between the two people. Even if there was tension before. Imagining another person as a happy individual getting what he or she wants to attract into their reality. More peace, laughter, and communication. And the difference between vibrations will be able to be noticed.

Many people working for an employer, or corporation, know what it's like when the boss is angry. Everyone around is walking on eggshells. Even worse, if this upset manager happens to direct the anger towards one specific employee, that employee will have to face the brunt of not only the anger but the accompanying humiliation as well. And humiliation is a horrible way to hurt and rob someone's energy. Consider it an act of violence.

In cases like these, it's really easy to be angry back at the boss and think of him or her in negative ways. This actually makes matters worse. That boss will sense the bad vibes and will further his or her tirade. The tension would be able to be cut with a knife.

Instead, the berated employee can think of this obviously unhappy person as a happy boss who is enjoying life. Usually, certain things about this boss will be known, including what he or she likes. So this employee can imagine his or her boss getting those things they desire.

The good news is that even if anyone feels a negative emotion, that person can use it to practice self-awareness. It is considered spiritual alchemy. Alchemy was a medieval practice where base metals were turned into gold. In this case, the base metal is the negative emotion, and the gold is the spiritual enlightenment that naturally comes with self-awareness. Being aware of the negative feeling is the perfect opportunity to observe it with a bird's eye view.

The following sailboat illustration will help explain how effortless it is once self-awareness is maintained and concentrated. A strong wind is caught in the sail of a boat, and this boat is easily gliding along and all the boatman has to do is steer. No strenuous effort, or trying to push or pull the sailboat in any way. That is what self-awareness does for someone gliding along with life situations.

Channels of Actions

Wallace D. Wattles, the author of the book *The Science of Getting Rich*, explains how the current existing things in the environment can help with the manifestation process. He wrote, "... this vision... sets all the creative forces at work IN AND THROUGH THEIR REGULAR CHANNELS OF ACTION, but toward you." Many manifestation methods mostly focus on non-physical action. Meaning that the thinking process and adjusting inner emotions can be considered an action, must a non-physical type of action. That may leave you wondering, "what actual physical action has to do with manifesting anyway?"

Wallace D. Wattles goes on to explain, "But you must act in a certain way, so that you can appropriate what is yours when it comes to you; so that you can meet the things you have in your picture, and put them in their proper places as they arrive." And the right things will arrive through synchronistic events that stand out like a neon sign. It is a matter of being prepared, ready for the reception of what is desired. Being consciously aware is how to get prepared for living a better life. Mr. Wattles sums this up by explaining, "By thought, the thing you want is brought to you; by action you receive it.

Every alternate reality is linked. Consciousness has everything to do with shifting realities. Every Universe has a corresponding observer. Nothing can exist or happen if there isn't a consciousness there to witness it. And all those conscious observers are linked to one overall conscious mind.

The one overall conscious mind is the eternal, multidimensional part of human-being. It is the one connection to any possible parallel universe. That is why it is so powerful to be aware of being aware. True self-awareness is recognizing the eternal divinity already existing within.

Consciousness is linked to physical matter the same way that steam, water, and ice are linked together. Steam, water, and ice are essentially the same thing but in different vibrational frequencies. In other words, consciousness and physical matter are one and the same. Just in different vibrational frequencies of energy. All is energy, it just seems like there is a separation of things because of how different those things vibrate in contrast to one another.

The density of physical matter is like ice. It is the vibrational frequency at its lowest. Water is not nearly as dense, and it can be comparable to the identity of an individual. And the highest vibration is like steam, which is similar to consciousness itself.

Taking any kind of action, any movement, no matter how mundane, is like riding a wave from the inner intention of the mind to the outer corresponding physical manifestation. The trick is to not take the action too seriously. Just take action for the sake of the action itself, at the moment. Follow the inspired action.

Chapter Five

The 1 to 5 Scale

"To know thyself is the beginning of wisdom."- Socrates

Now it's time to put together all that has been explained thus far in this book. Depending on your current vibrational level, the way you feel, certain manifestation methods are more appropriate than others. Getting too serious, as if way too important, creates more of a problem for you. So if you try to force yourself to think, feel and act in a certain way can conjure up more resistance and Murphy's Law.

It's better to start off slow. Like putting your car in neutral first before you drive. Shifting gears improperly can make you feel discomfort and anguish inside. The vibrational resistance will be felt. Self-awareness lets you know what gear, or vibe, your subconscious cruise control is in.

One- Relaxed Breathing

A scale of 1 to 5 is set up to help you figure out how to deal with certain thoughts, feelings, and situations. Whenever you are having a bad day and nothing can make you feel better, it is best to do nothing. If you can at the moment, go to bed and take a nap.

Or you can meditate. Just simply sit still and concentrate on your breathing and your heartbeat at the same time. Let the thoughts pass through your head as if they are clouds, don't get too attached to them. Relax every muscle in your body.

If you are in a situation where you don't have the luxury to just go rest your body, like being at work, just remember to breathe. Mental focus on your breath has a way of gently taming the energy of the Hermetic Pendulum's swing. Imagine your breath being the pendulum instead. In moments of stress, or being emotionally triggered, it can be hard to tame the reaction. Breathing is an easy thing to remember and to utilize for stress reduction.

Two- Spiritual Alchemy

The next level of vibrational frequency is also known as Spiritual Alchemy. Whatever situation that is bringing you down can be used for your benefit. After you have relaxed enough, you are ready for this level. And you will know whether or not if you are fully relaxed is by the way you feel. Notice the vibrational shift inside.

Look at the thought, person or situation in an impersonal way. Stare the fear right in the face in a relaxed state. Be nonreactive to the provocation. You'll know whether or not you are remaining impersonal by the way you feel. Stay fully relaxed and the negativity can't touch you.

A simple three-step process can help you with this. First, look at the unwanted thing impersonally. Second, notice the thoughts you have about that thing. And the final step is to be aware of the one who is thinking the thoughts about the thing.

To recap the process, it all starts with the awareness of the thing. Then noticing the thoughts about the thing. Then the realization of the thinker that is thinking the thoughts about the thing.

This process creates the necessary space for the solution to the problem to arise. Powerful inner intuitive insights will emerge within the mind. The signs and synchronicity will be a lot more emphasized for you. And that is the gold that comes out of the spiritual transmutation process. Of turning the base metal (unwanted thing) into gold (enlightenment.)

Three-The Flip Side

Now that you have faced your fears and realized there is nothing to fear at all, it's time for level 3 of the vibrational scale. The things that bother you have a flip side to it. It just takes your awareness to notice it.

The very thing that you think is so bad is actually helping you out. If you know what you don't want, then that means you now know exactly what you do want. Then your mind needs to focus on the positive side of things. And if there is a negative side of things, there must be a positive side.

"In the midst of chaos, there is also opportunity."- Sun Tzu. That quote is a perfect summary of the power of the Hermetic Principle of Rhythm and Polarity. The Hermetic Pendulum will eventually swing to a higher and better position. Just allow yourself to relax at the moment to notice it.

Four- Fix Your Thoughts

This level of vibration is where the momentum really starts to pick up. All you simply have to do is focus on the beautiful aspects you find appealing about either the world around you or your desire. It's a simple act of gratitude.

You can also focus on the beauty that is emphasized by the desire itself. If there is something you want to manifest, just focus on the qualities that stand out to you. Notice the energy of the vibrational frequency increasing as you do so. Simply focus on what you love about the intention.

It really doesn't matter what it is that you focus upon. As long as it gives you a good feeling, a positive inner reaction. Self-awareness will faithfully reveal it to you.

The quote from The Bible in Philippians 4:8, in the New Living Translation, is the best description of this level of vibrational frequency. And here it is for the second time in this book (it's worthy to be a mantra.) "Finally, brothers and sisters, whatever is true, whatever is noble, whatever is right, whatever is pure, whatever is lovely, whatever is admirable-- if anything is excellent or praiseworthy-- think about such things." Think about such things and notice the increased inner vibrational energy.

Another term for "fixing your thoughts" is Automatic Imagination. Allow your mind to run free and think about what it wants. As long as it is something that makes you feel good to think about. Let the STREAM of visualizations take on a life of their own. You'll be surprised by the insights they will give you.

It's a way to get intuitive guidance from the infinite intelligence of the Universe. Present a question or intention within your mind. Then close your eyes and enjoy the inner visuals that present themselves to you in your mind. Look for any metaphorical hidden messages.

Here is where the final Hermet Principle comes into effect. The Principle of Gender as described in the Kybalion as "Gender is in everything/ everything has its masculine and feminine principles; Gender manifests on all planes." In other words, the mind is the "male" force expressing out into the Universe. The Universe receives the "female," and is impressed by it. The roles are reversed whenever your mind is receiving expressions from the Universe. Such as signs, intuition, and synchronicity.

When you are "fixing your thought" you are the "male" dominate energy. When something external is taking over your mind, you are now in the "female" receptive mode. It is alright to be in the receptive mode when it comes to signs and synchronicity, but not when something else, like an energy vampire, is controlling your mind.

Five- The STREAM

The final level is called the STREAM. To recap what this acronym means, Sustain a Thought Repeatedly and Exemplify it in the Activities of the Moment. Belief is very well known to be powerful, many books discuss how it influences our lives. Another definition of belief is to sustain the same thought repeatedly. That's why it's so empowering to practice self-awareness, and the thoughts being held in the mind over and over again.

To exemplify the thought in the activities of the moment you simply recite a self-suggestion (stated in the present tense) as you perform an activity that correlates with the intention in mind. Here are some more examples that can be used on a day to day basis. The main metaphorical meanings to daily activities are used in this method such as driving, bathing, standing up, eating, drinking, breathing, using the bathroom, sleeping, turning on a light, opening a door and cleaning.

Driving-
Metaphorical Meanings- Inspiration, Strong Desire, Self-Mastery.
Affirmation- "I drive myself towards any intention I have in mind."

Bathing-
Metaphorical Meanings- Rebirth, Regeneration, Restoration.
Affirmation- "I regenerate myself and emerge as a new man/woman who succeeds no matter what."

Standing Up-
Metaphorical Meanings- Self-Assurance, Self-Confidence, Recognition.
Affirmation- " I stand up to adversity and reach my goals."

Eating-
Metaphorical Meanings- Absorption, Consuming, Satisfying.

Affirmation- "I satisfy the hunger I have for successful relationships with other people."

Drinking-
Metaphorical Meanings- Fulfilment, Absorption, Regeneration.
Affirmation- "I quench my thirst for knowledge that gets me ahead in life."

Breathing-
Metaphorical Meanings- Life, Absorption, Letting Go.
Affirmation- "I breath in more wealth and abundance and breath out unwanted fear about money."

Bathroom Break-
Metaphorical Meanings- Letting go, Removing.
Affirmation- "I let go of all self-limiting beliefs I have about myself that hold me back from success."

Sleeping-

Metaphorical Meanings- Rest, Renewal, Assurance.

Affirmation- "I rest in the assurance that all is well."

Turning on a Light (or anything else)-

Metaphorical Meanings- Energy, Understanding, Enlightenment

Affirmation- "I light up the world by successfully manifesting my intention."

Opening a Door-

Metaphorical Meaning- Opportunity, Freedom, Decision Making.

Affirmation- "I open the doors to success effortlessly."

Cleaning-

Metaphorical Meaning- Alignment, Balance, Clarifying, Purifying.

Affirmation- "I put things in their proper order to get things done."

These are just some general examples. The key is to make all this your own style.

Think of certain daily activities you can use for this process, and use your own words. Notice how certain activities and affirmations make you feel. And stick with the ones that feel the best.

Another way to STREAM into a preferred reality is to stay in the present moment and react in alignment with the person who is already living the intention successfully manifested. Mindfulness is very effective in manifesting desires. The confusion to some people is that they can't wrap their heads around the idea of being in the moment, and aiming for a goal at the same time. The present moment may seem to contain more lack than abundance and keeps their focus on what they don't have.

The now is the grand crossroad to infinite parallel universes. The goal you have in mind is an already existing reality, and the now is connected to it. In essence, because of your conscious awareness absorbed in that reality, you're already in that reality.

Certain life situations may cause a negative reaction, and therefore knock you off course towards living your best life. Anything involving money, personal relationships, and your career usually are the main areas of life that may spark a certain reaction out of you. Here is a list of the "forks in the road," either react negatively (left) or positively (right.)

The key here is to live life as if your already living in the desired reality, and you do that by reacting in alignment with that preferred reality. Imagine what happens immediately after the successful manifestation of your desire. What possible after-effects will there be if you made that goal a reality? What words would you say?

Money-
Former Reaction- "I never have enough."
New Reaction- "Wealth and abundance show up just like the ocean tides rise again."

Personal Relationships-

Former Reaction- "I'm not good enough for her/him."
New Reaction- "My sense of self-worth comes from me and me only."

Career-
Former Reaction- "I try so hard and nothing is happening for me."
New Reaction- "As long as I'm learning, I'm winning."

Conclusion

"The aim of art is to represent not the outward appearance of things, but their inward significance."- Aristotle

Nature and art both have a way of teaching profound Universal truths. Giving examples from nature on the manifestation process is a fitting way to conclude this book. All the art in the world can inspire a powerful shift in your mindset to manifest a better reality, by raising your vibrations.

The world is like a grand art gallery. Everyone is free to see what they wish to see. If there is a painting or sculpture you find repulsive, then simply look at something more pleasing to you. That is part of level 4 on a 1 to 5 Scale, fixing your thoughts on the beauty emphasized to you. By doing so you raise your vibrational frequency.

Look at the things in your life that you love. That rising vibrational frequency you're feeling within you is the feeling of love. If someone else doesn't love the same things you love, it's alright. They just don't like that particular piece of art.

Being out in nature has many benefits to the soul, and some of these benefits are guiding insights on how the Universe works and how to shift alternate realities. Raising energy to the next level of vibration tends to be the nature of all things in the Universe. As explained in the introduction, stars would vibrate to the next level and then produce a new element. Increasing rates of vibration are what manifests something new, it's the shift into an alternate Universe with that new element already existing.

The animal kingdom demonstrates the manifestation process in many ways. Caterpillars stay in their cocoon for a while and eventually manifest into a butterfly. It became a beautiful butterfly once the vibrations inside the cocoon reached the appropriate level.

Animals can sense vibrations from a possible predator from far away. The vibration coming from the animal and the vibrations coming from the predator are not in harmony with one another. This is why the prey can detect the predator. The different wavelengths from each animal are clashing with one another, and it is the clashing that is being felt.

The plant kingdom can also sense vibrations as well. Once the seed vibrates to the level of a sapling, it continues to grow to higher levels of vibrations and eventually grows to a full-grown tree. And this full-grown plant can also detect possible threats to its survival through the vibrations in the air. Plants also respond positively to positive vibrations as well.

Scientific research has reported the influence thought vibration has on plants. It is now called the Backster Effect. Dr. Backster attached electronic equipment to a plant in order to record any possible results from the science experiment. As soon as Dr. Backster entertained the thought to burn one of the leaves of the plant, the polygraph machine used to record any influence made on the plant went haywire.

Plants also have been known to react in a healthy way to good vibrations. Such as kind words and thoughts directed towards a plant, and relaxing classical music played near a plant. People with a green thumb may have a natural inclination to spread positive vibrations as they are gardening.

It is the light of conscious awareness that allows vibrations to be detected at all. And whenever any stress or drama is clouding your mind, the light of consciousness is always there. This is also displayed by Mother Nature through the phenomena of weather. No matter how dark, cold, cloudy and stormy it may be, the Sun is always shining above the clouds, which will eventually break through the clouds with its rays of light.

Printed in Great Britain
by Amazon